THE JOY FORMULA
THE SIMPLE EQUATION
THAT WILL CHANGE YOUR LIFE

MARY SCHILLER

Aptitude Consulting, LLC

www.joyformulabook.com

ISBN: 0692651497
ISBN-13: 978-0692651490

DEDICATION

To everyone who wants to experience true joy and inner peace.

CONTENTS

ACKNOWLEDGEMENTS

To my daughter, Rachel,
and my husband, Jeff,
for believing in me.

INTRODUCTION
ARE YOU READY FOR THIS?

You're about to hear a radical idea.

A radical idea about ...

JOY!

I'm talking about happiness multiplied by a thousand.

A deep, profound, undeniably beautiful feeling that encompasses all the other emotions and states of being we so desire: abundance, peace, connection, security and love.

I don't use the word "radical" lightly. What you're about to read is different from 99 percent of what else is out there about how to have more joy in your life. (Oh, and less fear, stress, anxiety, sadness and worry, too!)

Are you ready?

Here we go ...

Chapter 1
Why Aren't We Happier?

It was like a song stuck in my head, only worse.

"What's wrong with me? Why can't I just be happy?"

That was the refrain going through my mind in autumn of 2013, on a daily – sometimes hourly – basis.

You know that feeling of being seized by anxiety and worry, and it just won't go away no matter what you do?

It's not necessarily gripping you all the time, and sometimes you feel all right or even pretty good.

But that other feeling, the yucky one, is always there, rumbling beneath the surface like an earthquake about to shake you to your core. It's really annoying, to say the least. And at most, it can seem debilitating.

It was October of 2013 when I realized – more like admitted to myself – how desperate I actually felt. Even in situations when I should have been completely calm and relaxed, like when I went on vacation, that anxious lump in the gut was present.

Why? Well, at the time I believed there was something inside of me that was permanently broken, and I didn't know how to fix it.

All I desired was a deep feeling of peace and joy, and fewer feelings of anxiety and worry. I would have spent every penny I had if someone could've told me how to do that.

By all accounts, I should have been feeling really good at that point in my life. I had finished an intensive 16-month psychotherapy process for post-traumatic stress disorder (stemming from domestic violence in my first marriage many years earlier) and was doing a lot better than I had in a while.

My marriage (my second) was also improving. My husband and I had been traveling a rocky road for several years, but things between us were definitely on an upswing.

Instead of feeling good most of the time, however, I was feeling low-level anxiety just below the surface. I felt emotionally adrift, and I needed a life raft.

I know I'm not alone in those feelings – of wanting to have a greater sense of emotional well-being and happiness, of deep contentment and security.

On the surface, I had everything I needed: a roof over my head, food to eat, clothes to wear, a bit of money in the bank. I'm like most people in western culture. Would I like a few more creature comforts? Sure. Is the world perfect? No, and neither am I.

But still …

Why wasn't I happier?

Why aren't *we* happier?

At the end of 2013, I made a decision that I thought would lead to more happiness in my life.

In truth, it felt more like grasping at something, anything, to get myself back in the boat.

What did I do? I decided to become a life coach – because, well, isn't that logical, considering how great I felt at the time? (Yes, that was a sarcastic comment!)

I knew I had the skills to coach people based on my professional and personal experiences. I had survived some pretty tough trauma throughout my 20s and 30s, and I believed I could help others who had been through something similar, showing them that they weren't alone.

Simply put, I wanted to do something meaningful. That, to me, seemed like the key to real peace and joy in my life. So I enrolled in a coach-training program. At first, everything seemed fine. I liked the classes and what I was learning. A few weeks into the training, though, something began to feel "off" to me.

One day, on my lunch break from my job, I sat down next to a tree in Central Park.

I set up my iPhone, and I recorded a video to post on my then-fledgling coaching website. In that video, I shared a bit about my experience with domestic violence in my first marriage, and I remember stating that I finally saw that being happy was a choice.

Even while I was saying those words, they didn't ring true. But I didn't know what else to believe.

The psychotherapy process seemed to tell me the same thing, as was the entire self-development world and, certainly, the coach-training program I was in. The message was always something like this:

"Mary, you can be happy whenever you want to. You just have to change your thinking to be more positive, more present, more accepting of your life, and then you can choose to be happy."

UGH!

It just plain didn't work for me! I had tried all of that, and here I was trying to make other people do the same thing.

I went ahead and practiced the coaching techniques on a few people, but they didn't work nearly as well as I had hoped. I was letting them down, and I was also letting myself down.

And then, I came across a video in early 2014 that changed everything for me.

It showed me why I wasn't finding happiness where I had been looking for it.

And it showed me, for the first time, that happiness isn't a choice we have to make …

CHAPTER 2
THE MOMENT THAT ROCKED BROADWAY

One of the amusing things about the Internet is that it's such a rabbit hole. Click here, and you fall down one rabbit hole that leads to another and then another.

Well, one day I fell down the Internet rabbit hole and ended up watching a video of a woman describing a book she had read, called *The Inside-Out Revolution*. It was written by Michael Neill, and this woman, Nicola Bird, was explaining how much of an impact the book and the author had had on her life.

She was so earnest about it; she really was a compelling force, and I listened to the entire message. I didn't know exactly what she was talking about, but I knew one thing for sure. I had to buy the book.

I jumped onto Amazon and bought the Kindle version and the paperback, and then I went to Audible and bought the audiobook version, too. I started reading the Kindle book, and the next day on my subway commute to work, I began listening to the audiobook.

That same day, I took my usual lunchtime walk – except this time I went up Broadway instead of through Central Park – and continued listening to Michael Neill read *The Inside-Out Revolution*.

About thirty minutes into my walk, I stopped at an island in the middle of a big intersection near Lincoln Center and sat down on one of the benches there. The weather had begun to get warmer after a bleak winter, and there were pink and purple impatiens planted in the pots as a sign of spring about to arrive.

I sat and listened to the words in my ears, and I knew without doubt that I had found what I wanted most in life – joy, peace, success, security, fulfillment and love.

In that moment, life as I knew it stopped.

My world changed.

And not just a little, but everything fundamentally moved underneath my feet, as if Broadway itself had shifted direction.

It wasn't religion, philosophy or even deep spirituality. It was something completely different: something that I had never heard before.

I went back to my office, emailed the life coach training program and told them that I was quitting, and I've never looked back.

This short book will distill, in the most concise way that I can, what I've learned since that earthquake moment on Broadway near 66th Street – and I hope it will be as life changing for you as it has been for me.

I have named it the Joy Formula™ because that's how I have experienced all of this. It truly is a formula for joy – and for all of the beautiful emotions that human beings want to experience on a regular basis. It is so simple that sometimes when I share it with people, they are skeptical of its simplicity.

If you find yourself in that camp at first, it's quite all right. I believe it's because we are so conditioned to think that having a truly happy and joyful life, a successful life, requires a lot of effort – that having what we want requires struggle, hard work, suffering and stress that eventually lead to the good stuff.

In the next few pages, I'll reveal the Joy Formula™ to you.

The Joy Formula™ is based on the simplest equation you can imagine – which is good, since I'm terrible at math …

Chapter 3
Hold a "Mental Clearance Sale"

As I'm writing this book for you, I'm in the process of selling or giving away most of my personal possessions.

It's not because I'm following the trend of downsizing and simplifying one's life by getting rid of extra stuff. No, it's because my husband and I are planning to take an extended trip in an RV – perhaps a year or longer, starting sometime in 2016. We don't intend to keep our primary residence, so we're going to sell it, too. And we don't want to pay to store a lot of our belongings.

So what does all this have to do with a book about a formula for joy? Well, in going through the process of tossing things I don't need or want anymore, I realized that for almost two years I've been doing something similar in my life, as a whole – only without all the back-breaking work and numerous garbage bags.

The results have been no less than astonishing.

Even when I was dealing with post-traumatic stress disorder for all those years (more than 30 years, actually), I still had times when I felt at least somewhat at peace and joyful. The feelings were there, but they were fleeting.

The problem was, I didn't know where they were coming from or how to re-create them on a regular basis. I made an assumption that something I was doing was creating joy, or that some person was responsible for the feeling – like my daughter or another loved one. I chased after the feelings, but they seemed elusive to me. They wouldn't "stick."

It wasn't until I read and listened to Michael Neill's book that I saw what was actually going on.

In the past, I had been focusing on adding things into my life to create a feeling of joy and also trying – via all sorts of techniques – to obliterate everything that wasn't joyful. Wow, did I ever have it wrong! Innocently wrong, but still wrong.

What did I try to do to be more joyful? For starters ...

• Tapping (also known as "Emotional Freedom Technique," or EFT)
  • Psychotherapy (I lost count at 25 different therapists)
  • Subliminal messages
  • Self-hypnosis
  • The other kind of hypnosis
  • Relaxation techniques
  • Yoga
  • Neuro Linguistic Programming ("NLP")
  • All kinds of other mental "tricks"
  • Meditation

Let's look at meditation as an example.

Since I had such troubling thoughts related to post-traumatic stress disorder (PTSD), I thought meditation could help me stop having these thoughts. Well, I couldn't control or stop my thinking no matter how long I tried to meditate. I would lie on a purple yoga mat on the floor of the bedroom and see my thoughts going by, but they were all still there and still troubling. Eventually I quit meditating, feeling like a failure.

I also tried to feel more joyful by engaging in activities that, on the surface, seemed like they were happiness generators. Like what?

How about these potential happiness generators …?

- Knitting
- Swimming
- Walking outdoors regularly
- Taking photographs
- Spending more time with my family
- Removing myself from stressful situations
- Staying away from "toxic" people

And on and on. But you know what I figured out?

- Knitting didn't make me happy.
- Swimming didn't make me happy.
- Walking outdoors didn't make me happy.
- Taking photographs didn't make me happy.

• Spending time with my family didn't make me happy.

• Removing myself from stressful situations or staying away from "toxic" people didn't make me happy.

Here's the confusing part. These activities, tricks, tools and techniques seemed, at times, like they actually worked!

I felt happy while doing them – but only sometimes. Other times, I didn't. Sometimes, I'd go out to take photographs and just feel blah. Or I'd spend time with my daughter and worry about her future instead of enjoying her company.

What activities are you doing in order to try to bring more happiness – more joy – into your life? Write them here or on a piece of paper.

Oh, yes. Then there were all the things I thought I *needed* in my life in order to be happy. Like what? Well …

- A super-duper passionate marriage
- Good health
- Wonderful, meaningful work
- Excellent friendships
- More money in the bank (of course, right?)

What do you think you need in your life in order to be happy? Write your ideas here or on another piece of paper.

Now it's time for you to hold a "mental clearance sale," just as I have.

But this is the easiest activity of all, because it requires no work whatsoever. You don't have to gather up all your old thinking, mindsets, beliefs, techniques, tools or strategies and recycle them or take them to the dump.

So ...

If you're searching for the right way to think in order to make your life better, *you can stop now.*

If you're searching for the perfect techniques, tools and tricks to make your life more joyful, successful and secure, *you can stop now.*

If you're looking for a step-by-step solution to feeling happier and less anxious, more peaceful and less worried, *you can stop now.*

If you're doing anything at all to "make yourself happy," *you can stop now* (but continue doing what you enjoy, just for its own sake).

If you're having a running dialogue in your head, berating yourself for this, that and the other thing, *you can stop now.*

Stop, and look over here …

CHAPTER 4
THE JOY FORMULA™

Glance at the magazine rack at your supermarket or read some of your favorite self-help or self-development websites or blogs. What article headlines about happiness do you see? Here are five results of a quick Google search that I did just this very minute:

- "40 Ways to be Happy"
- "7 Steps to Becoming a Happier Person"
- "The 15 Habits of Incredibly Happy People"
- "8 Life-Changing Lessons from TED Talks on How to be Happy"
- "10 Scientifically Proven Ways to be Incredibly Happy"

They all sound good, right? Logical? Typical? Normal?

They're all wrong. Wow, did I just say that? You bet I did!

They are all approaching happiness from the wrong direction. I did the exact same thing for nearly my entire life.

I'm about to share the simple equation that's going to change your life forever. First, however, a quick trip to a fine restaurant ...

I'm fortunate enough to have enjoyed a couple of meals at a magnificent restaurant in New York City called Jean Georges. I'm not a "foodie," but I love the meals served by the chefs at Jean Georges. They choose the freshest ingredients, all at their prime, sparkling moments of taste, and combine them to create true works of art for the palate.

In a similar way, I thought I had to combine the ingredients of life in the most perfect way possible in order to feel happier.

I thought I had to have the perfect friends, the perfect spouse, the perfect neighborhood, the perfect career, the perfect attitude, the perfect daily routine, the perfect meditation techniques, the perfect mindset, the perfect way to think about things in life, and so on.   I thought I had to control my thinking, develop my mental muscles, have the 7 habits of those highly successful people, empower myself, model my life after those I admired, take leaps of faith, believe in myself, have more self-confidence, adopt a positive outlook, see the glass as half full, deal with my "issues," and so forth.

What books have you read or programs have you taken to try to improve your life? Write them here or on a separate piece of paper.

I know this may be hard to believe right now, but we don't need to do any of that in order to feel joy, peace, contentment, and security and enjoy more success than we ever thought possible. In fact, doing all of that stuff is actually keeping us away from the feelings we want.

It's not an "adding" of things that allows us to feel joy.

It's a taking away.

Here is the equation.

Joy = You – An Innocent Misunderstanding

What is this innocent misunderstanding? Well, it's a two-part answer.

1. Our biggest misunderstanding in life is believing that our experience comes from anything other than our thinking in the moment.

Take a minute or two and read that sentence again.

Read it aloud a few times.

Our biggest misunderstanding in life is believing that our experience comes from anything other than our thinking in the moment.

This is not a small thing I'm asking you to see. To say it another way, our thinking doesn't just influence the way we experience things in life. It actually creates that experience.

For example, someone gets angry with us, and we feel hurt. We assume that the person or the person's anger made us feel hurt.

But it doesn't work that way.

What makes us feel hurt is our own thinking in that moment.

Another example: We go on vacation and feel happy. We believe that the vacation, the environment, the activities and the people are making us feel happy.

But it doesn't work that way.

What makes us feel happy is our thinking in that moment.

Thought comes first. Then comes our experience. It works this way all the time, all day long, whether we're aware of it or not.

I used to believe that my experience came first, and then my thinking influenced the way I felt about that experience. I thought that the chain of events looked something like this:

An experience → My thinking → My feelings →
My actions → Results

But that isn't how it works at all. It's how it appears to us, for sure, but that appearance is false. It's an illusion that our thinking creates, and it can look totally real to us.

Here's how things used to look to me in relation to my old job, for instance:

Being in the office → "I hate this place" → Frustration and anger → I did the bare minimum → I got a mediocre performance review, which led me to thinking, "I hate this place." With this new understanding of how life really works, I then saw the same job this way:

My thinking about my job $\rightarrow$ My experience of my job

End of equation.

Does this mean that I have to change my thinking in order to have a better experience? Because that's how it seems, right?

We're told that we have to think positively about things, be "present" and so forth, and that's what will change our experience.

Well, guess what? That's all wrong, too.

Not only isn't it necessary to do any of that, as I mentioned a moment ago, it's actually keeping us feeling worse.

Remember that mental clearance sale I talked about earlier? This is what I mean. There is no need to try to change or control our thinking, because no one can do that.

We can't control what thoughts pop into our head. The more we try, the worse it gets. The more we try to "change our mindset" or "think positively" or any number of other techniques, the more stuck in our thinking we become. Thought is designed to flow through us like a stream. How much effort does it take to make a stream change direction? You'd have to build the Hoover Dam!

Yet that's what most of us try to do every minute of every day when we believe that the answer to feeling happier, to becoming more successful or being less stressed is to change our mindset, think positively, be more present in the moment and so on.

Thought flows in, thought flows out. It's what it's designed to do. It's what creates our experience in every single moment, whether we're awake or asleep.

And what are our feelings?

Our feelings simply reflect our thinking in the moment – nothing more, nothing less.

I used to think my feelings were giving me important information about my life. I was wrong!

Our feelings don't tell us anything: they don't predict

anything, don't reveal anything. They're a mirror of our thinking, and that is all. As Michael Neill writes, "We're living in the feeling of our thinking."

So let's return to the misunderstanding and tie this together.

The misunderstanding is that it looks like things on the outside of us are causing our experience every day.

The boss gets mad at us. There's a traffic jam and we're late. Our spouse doesn't do enough around the house. Our friends didn't invite us to the party. We get a medical test result that's not what we want to hear. We're scared to do public speaking. We feel good when we're in someone's company. We relax on vacation. We feel inspired by listening to a speaker. And a million other examples. We assume that all of these "outside" events and people create our feelings.

They do not. Only our thinking does that.

Everything we experience in life – even the things we physically touch – come to us via thought.

"All you have to know is that everything is created from thought. You don't have to know anything else."

Sydney Banks, the person who first expressed all of this as the Three Principles

I'll let you digest that statement by Sydney Banks for a moment or two.

So if we don't have to do anything about our thinking, then what do we do? People ask me this question often, and I understand why. We're so conditioned to believe that we have to do something in order to make our lives better, to feel better, to be happier, more productive, more inspired and what have you.

But all you need to do is open your eyes and look in this new direction. See that you think. See that your thinking is creating your moment-to-moment experience of life. There is nothing for you to do, nothing for you to change.

Just see that you think, and see that it creates your experience – not that it merely influences it, but actually creates it.

"There's nothing on the outside that can help you.
And there's nothing on the outside that can hurt you.
Because there is no outside."

Sydney Banks

When you're ready, you can move on to the second part of this misunderstanding, which relates closely to the first ...

2. We don't realize that we're actually made of the thing we're trying so hard to experience: peace, love, security, creativity and joy – and every other emotion that gives us a beautiful feeling.

Every single person has innate mental health and well-being.

I'll repeat that, because it's so meaningful and goes against pretty much everything we're taught to think about each other and ourselves.

You have innate mental health and well-being.

It's ever present and unchanging. Nothing can ever touch it, harm it, crack it or tarnish it. No matter what happens on the "outside," we are never truly harmed, ever.

When I saw this, that I had innate health and well-being that was untouched from the moment I came into this world, it was a life-changing moment for me.

Do you remember earlier, when I said that I believed a part of me was permanently broken because of the domestic violence, trauma and PTSD I experienced? When I realized that that wasn't true at all, that nothing had touched who I really was, the light came on and has never gone off.

I heard those words, and I immediately knew it was true, because even in the midst of PTSD, I was sometimes happy. I sometimes felt good.

If I had been permanently broken, how could I have ever felt times of real peace and joy? It wasn't because in those times I was "doing" all the right things. It was simply that in those times, I was living life as my true self – the self that wasn't listening to all the PTSD-related thoughts that floated through my mind.

When I realized my mistake, I saw that I didn't even have to watch those thoughts go by, didn't have to acknowledge them or worry about them at all. I could feel anxious or whatever but not worry, because that feeling reflected only my thinking in that moment. It didn't reflect who I was or even indicate the quality of my life.

After a while, those PTSD-type thoughts (and many other thoughts) turned into sort of a low hum that I no longer paid attention to, until they disappeared nearly altogether.

A quote attributed to St. Francis of Assisi says, "What you're looking for is what you're looking with."

Read that again: *"What you're looking for is what you're looking with."*

All those years I spent searching for joy, wanting to bring it into my life somehow, I was actually looking to things *outside* of me instead of *inside* of me.

All that time, I was searching not just for something that I already had, but that I already *was*.

When you get caught up in your thinking and you believe it's all real, you're simply forgetting for a moment who you really are.

In those times, look past your thinking. See that you're thinking, know that it's creating your experience, but look past it to the source of that mighty mountain stream.

34

Joy = You – An Innocent Misunderstanding

What happens when we remove this misunderstanding from the equation?

Joy = You

This! Could this be any more magnificent?

You are joy brought to life.

You are made of it. It's your birthright, the stuff that makes up who you are. If you wanted to run away from joy for some reason, you couldn't because it's what you're made of. Even in times when you feel down, you are still made of joy. Even in times when you feel the most intense emotions, like grief or anger, you are still made of joy.

"Then why can't I feel joyful all the time, Mary?" you might ask.

Consider the first part of this misunderstanding: that we aren't seeing where our experience is really coming from. We're listening to our thinking and believing it's real.

We're looking to things and people on the "outside" and seeing them as the cause of our state of being.

Once we see even a glimpse of this new understanding – that everything we experience is coming from our own thinking – it's like our thoughts get released from behind the Hoover Dam, and all the joy that we're made of comes rushing back up to the surface of our lives.

Joy = You – An Innocent Misunderstanding

The misunderstanding:

1. Believing that our experience comes from anything other than our thinking in the moment.

2. Not realizing that we're actually made of the thing we're trying so hard to feel: peace, security, abundance, love, joy.

How will knowing the Joy Formula™ change your life?

Let's see …

CHAPTER 5
HOW KNOWING THE JOY FORMULA™
CAN CHANGE YOUR LIFE FOR THE BETTER

To change my life, I used to think that I had to …

• "Make things happen"

• "Work smarter, not harder"

• "Stay focused on the goal"

• "Develop a plan of attack"

• "Follow a step-by-step program"

• "Improve daily habits"

• "Live in the present moment"

… and on and on. Read most self-development books and articles, and you'll see that they all (or almost all) have something that they're telling us we have to do in order to really change our lives.

The Joy Formula™ doesn't tell you to do anything. It tells you to *stop* doing.

Instead, simply see that you have been innocently living with a misunderstanding about where your experience is actually coming from and who you really are.

We all have them, those moments when we can feel blind to this truth. What do we do then?

When I feel myself getting worked up about something or when I feel low, that's when I know I'm believing the illusion that something on the "outside" is causing me a problem.

In those moments, I'll sometimes stop and ask, "Am I seeing that this thing is thought created, or am I not?"

If I'm not, you know what I do?

Nothing! I don't worry about it. I just keep going. I look past my thinking to who I really am: a being who has infinite resources at my disposal.

You can then begin to see your thinking as inconsequential, because 99 percent of the time, our personal thinking isn't telling us much that's useful.

In those moments of peace, of real joy, your thinking is slowed down, quieted down, to the point where you can't really hear it anymore – like static on the radio that has been turned down, and now you can hear the brilliant, natural symphony of your real nature's birdsongs all around you.

Here's another thing that amuses me to no end.

If, for example, I appear to be worried about money (or whatever), I'll sometimes say to myself, "I don't have a money problem, I have a thinking problem."

And then I realize, with a huge sigh of relief and usually a belly laugh, that I don't have to do anything about that thinking problem!

All I need to do is see that my thinking is creating that experience for me. Period. Full stop.

Fill in the blanks for yourself about a few things, here or on a separate piece of paper:

"I don't have a _____ problem, I have a thinking problem."

"I don't have a _____ problem, I have a thinking problem."

"I don't have a _____ problem, I have a thinking problem."

"I don't have a _____ problem, I have a thinking problem."

"I don't have a _____ problem, I have a thinking problem."

So much has changed for me in the past two-plus years since I found what I've called the Joy Formula™.

These milestones have come not from striving or working hard, but from stopping everything I had been doing before.

I now understand that if something seems like effort, I'm looking in the wrong direction and just need to turn my head slightly to remember who I really am – and what resources are available to me.

Here are some tangible examples from my own life of how the Joy Formula™ has made a difference:

• I finished writing my first novel in about eight weeks' time (nearly 50,000 more words!) after it had sat dormant for almost three years.

• As of this writing, I have spent the past year with my daughter who lives abroad. This is something I had worked really hard to "make happen" (because I've really missed her) and instead, the situation changed without my doing anything.

• I quit my job of eight years after trying to leave it for five years, with no luck at all.

• People are turning up in my life and wanting to help me in several areas, like business, without my even asking them.

• I now spend the majority of my time doing things I enjoy.

- My husband and I are making fun plans for our future together.

- I have no more symptoms of post-traumatic stress disorder and far fewer nightmares, which used to happen several times a week.

- I've been able to connect with and teach people what I'm writing about in this book.

What changes would you like to see in your own life? And when would you like to see them happen?

Write a few ideas here or on another piece of paper:

I know that it can seem impossible to change certain things about your life. I felt that way, too.

In my case, I thought that I would always deal with symptoms of PTSD and that I'd never feel truly, deeply happy. I believed that something was fundamentally wrong with me.

Thanks to the Joy Formula™ that I've shared with you, the whole world has opened up to me. Things that once seemed impossible, like finishing my novel, connecting with extraordinary people on a regular basis and talking to you about joy, are now part of my everyday life.

Do less. When something feels like effort, *stop*.

Look in this new direction, instead.

Joy = You – An Innocent Misunderstanding

The misunderstanding:

1. Believing that our experience comes from anything other than our thinking in the moment.

2. Not realizing that we're actually made of the thing we're trying so hard to feel: peace, security, abundance, love, joy.

You must have questions, right? Here are some answers …

CHAPTER 6
FREQUENTLY ASKED QUESTIONS

Q. Is this like the Law of Attraction?

A. No. All you need "do" is see that you're thinking, and that your thinking is creating your experience. Once you see that nothing outside of you is creating your moment-to-moment experience, the misunderstanding is gone. You don't have to try to change or control your thinking in any way.

The second part of the misunderstanding clears up the mistaken idea that we have attract good feelings and abundance into our lives. Why would we have to attract something that we already are? The answer is that we don't!

We already have everything. We already *are* everything.

Q. Did you come up with the Joy Formula™ all on your own, Mary?

A. The Joy Formula™ is my interpretation of the insights of Sydney Banks and his expression of those insights as the Three Principles of Mind, Consciousness and Thought. I've personally called it the Joy Formula™ because every time this misunderstanding is removed – every time I see that my thinking is creating my experience, and not something else – I'm back to feeling joyful again.

This is how this *new* understanding has felt to me: as if the misunderstanding is slowly dissolving away, so I now feel much more like my true self, which is made of joy, creativity, light, wisdom … all those wonderful things.

Q. What really makes the Joy Formula™ – based on the Three Principles you mentioned – so different?

A. It is not prescriptive. It is descriptive. It is not telling us to do anything. It is simply showing us what is really going on. Once we see how things work, we can begin living with true freedom and, of course, more joy.

Q. So if I don't have to do anything, well ... I'm confused. Then what do I do?

A. Nothing. You have innate health and well-being. When you see that there is nothing outside of you creating your experience, and that it's all coming from within you, it's like you've pressed the "reset" button on your whole system. Your system is always tilting in the direction of health. In other words, even though you're not aware of it, you are always conspiring to help ... you!

Q. If I understand the Joy Formula™, does that mean I'll never feel sad, anxious or fearful or that I'll never have low moods again?

A. You'll still have those feelings sometimes because that's part of the human experience. We have thoughts; those thoughts instantly create certain feelings.

But here's the difference: you don't need to worry about having those feelings because they're simply reflecting your thinking in the moment, and that's all.

Your feelings don't mean anything more than that. They're not a reflection of who you are or how well or badly your life is going. They don't reflect you, because you are much, much bigger than your thoughts and feelings.

Your feelings only ever do that one thing: reflect thought in the moment. Feel the feeling, whatever it is, and wait it out. Don't be afraid of it. It can't hurt you. A new feeling will come along in a moment, and when you're in this space of understanding instead of misunderstanding, it will be a more beautiful feeling when it arrives.

Q. Who have been your biggest influences – people whose work I should read or listen to?

A. I owe a huge debt of gratitude first and foremost to the late Sydney Banks, who first expressed this paradigm as the Three Principles (upon which my teaching is based).

Although they don't know that I'm mentioning them, Michael Neill has been a huge part of my learning journey, as have Jamie Smart, George Pransky, Linda Pransky, Jenny and Rudi Kennard, and other practitioners who have brought this understanding into my life. And I can't forget Nicola Bird, whose video I saw that day.

What is the next step? Let's …

Chapter 7
Share the Joy

People deserve to feel more joy in their lives – including you and those you love and care about. It's my dream to share this simple formula with as many people as possible because I truly believe that the world can be a happier and more peaceful place. You can help me share the joy around the globe just by telling one person about The Joy Formula™.

1. Your review of this short book on Amazon or wherever you purchased it (thank you!) would be so appreciated. Many, many thanks.

2. If *The Joy Formula* has been valuable to you, please share the joy in a post, blog or tweet, or give a copy of this book to a

friend or loved one. You might find people in your workplace, your neighborhood, your place of worship or your child's school who could benefit, too.

3. Join me online at www.joyformulabook.com for more resources and to get in touch with me. I'd love to have a conversation with you about having more joy and ease in life.

Thank you for reading and sharing *The Joy Formula*.

Much love to you,

Mary

NOT THE END,
BECAUSE THERE IS NO END TO JOY

ABOUT THE AUTHOR

Mary Schiller is a success and well-being specialist and writer who helps people experience more joy, relaxation and clarity in their lives.

Before she began teaching people the Joy Formula™, Mary taught university students how to write the perfect essay. Later, she became a communications officer at Columbia University, crafting messages for the business and medical schools. She holds advanced degrees in English and in education.

A native Californian, Mary loves the sun and the surf but also enjoys traveling to Paris and sampling every delicacy in the patisserie. She's passionate about classical music (Beethoven is unmatched), art, photography and knitting, particularly sweaters. She's married and has a grown daughter plus two adorable cats. While Mary and her husband currently live in New York City, they plan to take an extended cross-country trip in an RV, so she can take *The Joy Formula* on the road.

Find Mary online at www.joyformulabook.com. She also has a blog at www.thedailyprinciples.com, and her email address is mary@thedailyprinciples.com.

21527221R00036

Printed in Great Britain
by Amazon